# THE WONDERS OF EGYPT

## A COURSE IN EGYPTOLOGY

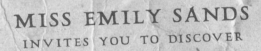

MISS EMILY SANDS
INVITES YOU TO DISCOVER

THE TREASURES OF
ANCIENT EGYPT

SPECIAL TICKET
ADMIT ONE
ACCESS UNLIMITED

GIZA PLATEAU AND THE GREAT PYRAMIDS

GIZA PLATEAU AND THE

GIZA PLATEAU AND THE

GIZA PLATEAU AND THE GREAT PYRAMIDS

# PATSY'S
## tours

including the
### Giza Plateau
and the
### Great Pyramids

The Sphinx, left, stands
guard over the Giza Plateau.
A colossal statue with the
body of a lion and the head of
a man, it has been twice buried
and twice rescued from the
shifting sands. Around
1490 BC it was uncovered by
the royal prince who was to
become King Thutmosis IV,
and in AD 1925 it was
uncovered again by French
engineer Emile Baraize.

## Walk Like An Egyptian!

### On A 'Rambling Rameses' Walking Tour Of Egypt.

Available November – February, From Cairo to Luxor and Back.

This edition produced in 2005 by
TEMPLAR PUBLISHING,
An imprint of The Templar Company plc,
Pippbrook Mill, London Road, Dorking, Surrey, RH4 1JE, UK
Text and design copyright © 2005 by The Templar Company Plc.
Illustration copyright © 2005 by Ian Andrew,
Nick Harris and Helen Ward
Designed by Jonathan Lambert and Nghiem Ta
ALL RIGHTS RESERVED.
First Edition.
ISBN 1-84011-882-2
Manufactured in China

Publisher's note: According to the editors, LIZ FLANAGAN and
DUGALD STEER, when the publisher received the manuscript of
"Egyptology – Search for the Tomb of Osiris" from Joanna
Sutherland in 2004, it was thought that no further works by
Miss Emily Sands, who went missing on an expedition up the
Nile in 1927, would be forthcoming. But it now appears that
one of the detectives hired by Lady Farncombe to investigate
the Sands disappearance did actually uncover another book,
which Emily had been preparing for her niece and nephew.
However, since the publisher still cannot say for certain
that a Miss Sands ever existed, readers must decide
for themselves whether the story is true or
simply an elaborate concoction.

www.egyptology1926.com

templar publishing

*One of the Colossi of Memnon, West Bank, Luxor*
*Built around 1360 BC by King Amenhotep III.*

# The Wonders of Egypt

## PART 1: THE HISTORY OF ANCIENT EGYPT

## PART II: LIFE AND CULTURE IN ANCIENT EGYPT

## PART III: GODS AND RELIGION IN ANCIENT EGYPT

## APPENDICES

This photograph shows the members of my "Egyptology" expedition standing in front of the pyramids.

A photograph of the temple of the crocodile god Sobek at Kom Obo.

You can add these Egyptian stamps to your collection.

The "Bennu Bird"
27th December 1926

My Dearest Niece and Nephew,

   I am very sorry that I will not be able to come and
see you during the Christmas holidays, I do so look
forward to the lovely time we spend together each year.
As you know from the postcard which I sent from Luxor,
I am having an exciting time leading an expedition that
is going up the River Nile in Egypt, looking for a lost
tomb.  I am travelling on an old-fashioned sailing
barge called the "Bennu Bird". Although we spend most
mornings visiting ancient tombs and temples, I still
have quite a lot of time on my hands. So as well as
writing a journal of my expedition, I have written a
book to teach you all about Ancient Egypt.

   I expect that I shall be in Egypt until March or
April — but if all goes well, it could be longer.
I must stop writing now because my boat is just about
to dock at Edfu, near the famous Temple of Horus.
Do say a big "Hello" to Lady Amanda for me, if you see
her, and to Mummy and Daddy, too. Let them know I shall
send a card as soon as I have more news!

   Your loving Aunt,

   Emily

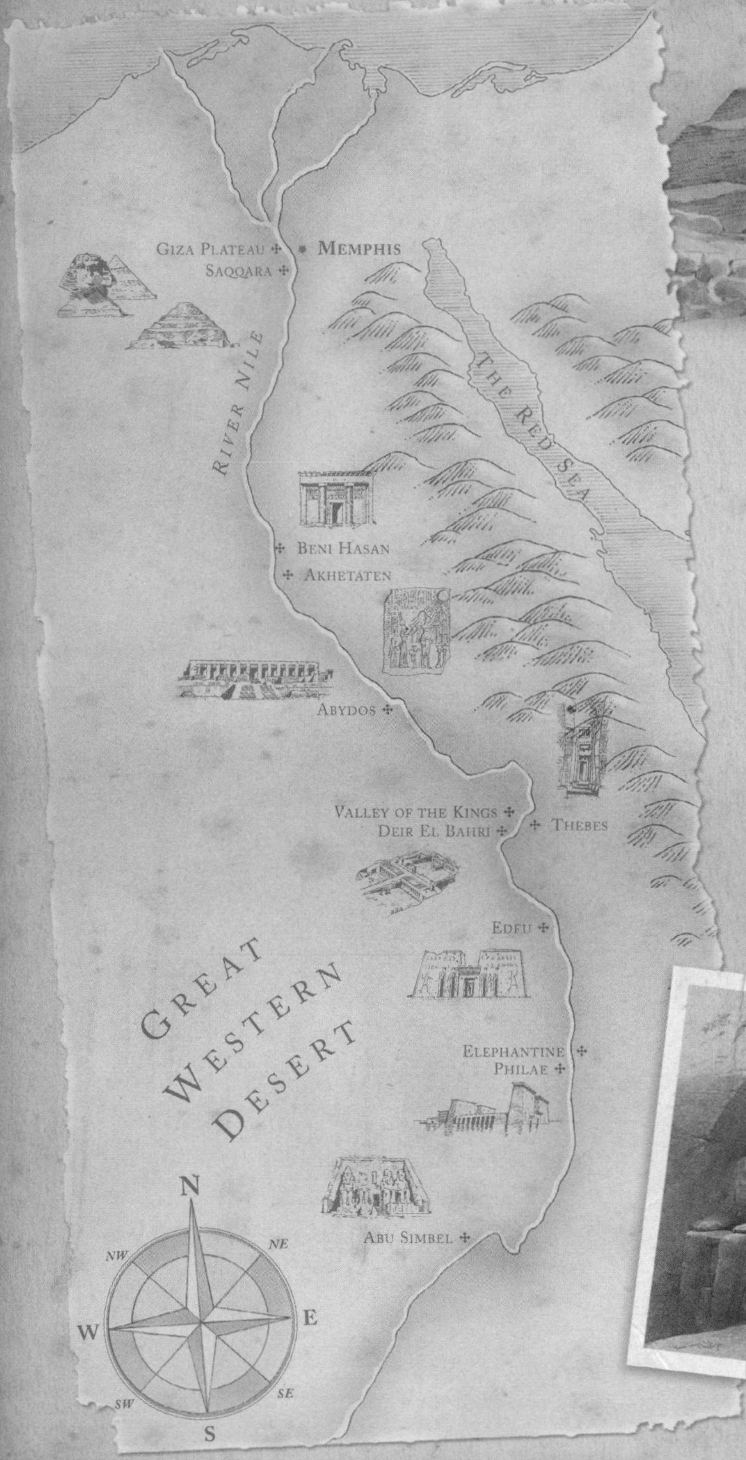

GIZA PLATEAU ✛ • MEMPHIS
SAQQARA ✛

*RIVER NILE*

*THE RED SEA*

✛ BENI HASAN
✛ AKHETATEN

ABYDOS ✛

VALLEY OF THE KINGS ✛
DEIR EL BAHRI ✛  ✛ THEBES

EDFU ✛

ELEPHANTINE ✛
PHILAE ✛

GREAT
WESTERN
DESERT

ABU SIMBEL ✛

N
NW    NE
W         E
SW    SE
S

*Hypostyle Hall, Karnak*

*Temple of Rameses II, Abu Simbel*

# Part I

# The History of Ancient Egypt

Nearly five thousand years ago, the lands that lay along the northernmost part of the river Nile were united for the first time under a single king known as Narmer. Believed by his people to be a living god, Narmer was the first of many hundreds of Pharaohs under whose rule the land of Egypt became home to one of the most impressive civilisations the world has ever known. As you can see in the Chronology of Egyptian History on pages 74 and 75, it was a culture that would last in a substantially similar form for more than three thousand years.

Obelisk of Thutmosis I

*Concerning Egypt itself I shall extend my remarks to a great length, because there is no other country that possesses so many wonders, nor any that has such a number of works that defy description.*
"The Histories", Herodotus, 440 BC

# Lesson 1
## The Origins of Egypt: Up to 2650 BC

Egypt, with its fertile soil, was home to people thousands of years before the Pharaohs. Archaeologists have found traces of people who settled into communities, and the evidence of their fine pottery, jewellery and flint tools shows us how skilled they were. These people began farming and domesticating animals. They also began to wage war as they fought for control of this prized strip of land on the banks of the great river Nile.

According to some historical sources, Narmer, a king from Hieraconpolis, unified Upper Egypt, the part of Egypt which lies south of modern Cairo, with Lower Egypt, the part which lies to the north of Cairo and takes in the Nile Delta. The first historical king of Egypt, he founded the first of more than thirty dynasties of Egyptian kings. His reign began around the year 2900 BC.

*Right: This palette shows King Narmer defeating an enemy. Some people believe that it commemorates the unification of Egypt.*

*Left: A golden hawk's head from Hieraconpolis.*

## LEGENDARY ORIGINS

The Ancient Egyptians believed that the king who united Egypt
and founded its capital at Memphis was called Menes. Whether
Menes was the same person as Narmer or a legend created from
stories about several kings, no one knows.

*WhiteCrown*

*Red Crown*

*From earliest times, the king
of Egypt wore a crown that
symbolised his rule over the
two parts of Egypt. This
double crown was made by
joining the traditional white
crown of Upper Egypt to the
red crown of Lower Egypt.*

*Double Crown*

ACTIVITY: You can see from the chronology on pages 74–75 that Ancient
Egyptian history is divided into three main periods: the Old Kingdom,
the Middle Kingdom and the New Kingdom. Here are the names of some
important Old Kingdom kings, along with the dates they ruled.
Can you put them in order, oldest first?

| | | | |
|---|---|---|---|
| Khaefra | 2520–2494 BC | Menkaura | 2490–2472 BC |
| Snefru | 2575–2551 BC | Khufu | 2551–2528 BC |
| Djedefra | 2528–2520 BC | | |

ANSWERS: Snefru, Khufu, Djedefra, Khaefra, Menkaura

# The Old Kingdom: 2650 to 2450 BC

The kings of Egypt's first royal dynasties were very powerful. Treated as a living god, the king was seen as the only person who could speak to the gods and ensure peace and stability throughout the land. To understand the strength and influence of these Old Kingdom kings, you have only to look at their greatest legacy, which still dominates the Egyptian landscape: the pyramids. The famous pyramids at Giza didn't spring from the imagination of an Egyptian architect perfectly formed. Instead, there were several stages of development as various kings experimented with different styles of tomb.

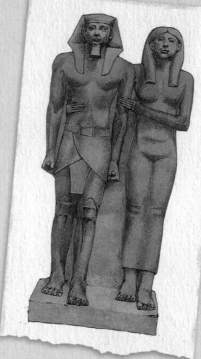

*A statue of an Old Kingdom Pharaoh: King Menkaura and Queen Khamererenebty.*

*The illustrations below show the rise and fall in the height of the pyramids. King Snefru was the most prolific builder. He had three pyramids constructed — two based on a stepped design and a third 'true' pyramid.*

| Step Pyramid of Zoser, 2630 BC 204ft. (62m.) | Pyramid of Meidum, Snefru, 2600 BC 306ft. (92m.) | Bent Pyramid, Snefru, 2600 BC 344ft. (105m.) | Red Pyramid, Snefru, 2600 BC 341ft. (104m.) |

Egypt's dry sands have kept many secrets over the years. Lift the flaps to excavate these mounds in the desert.

ACTIVITY: Near the pyramid of Khaefra lies a huge sculpture called the Sphinx. This sculpture has the head of a man and the body of a lion and lay covered by sand for centuries. See how much you can find out about the Sphinx in your local library.

*Great Pyramid of*
*Khufu, 2550 BC*
*481ft. (147m.)*

*Pyramid of*
*Khaefra, 2520 BC*
*471 ft. (144m.)*

*Pyramid of*
*Menkaura, 2490 BC*
*213ft. (65m.)*

# *Memphis and Saqqara*

The kings of the Old Kingdom needed a city that was majestic enough to suit them, and central enough to control the whole of the country. They built Memphis on the river Nile near the point where Upper and Lower Egypt met. It was a well-chosen site for a powerful city that would often be used as the capital by Egypt's kings over the next 3,000 years.

ACTIVITY: The Pharaoh has ordered you to build a new city. Which of these sites is the best place to build?

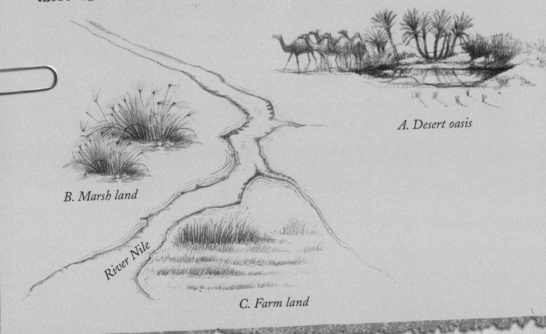

A. Desert oasis

B. Marsh land

River Nile

C. Farm land

ANSWER: The best place to build a city is on the farm land, near enough to the river so that goods can be moved easily by boat. There may not be enough water at the oasis to sustain a large city, while the marshland is too wet and is likely to flood.

## SAQQARA

At Saqqara, to the west of the new city of Memphis, the kings and nobles built their enormous tombs. It was there that King Zoser commissioned his royal architect Imhotep to build the world's first monumental stone building – the Step Pyramid.

*Right, King Zoser's Step Pyramid was surrounded by a large wall that enclosed temples and courtyards.*

1. Step Pyramid
2. Courtyard
3. Heb-Sed Court
4. Storerooms
5. Funerary Temple & Pyramid Entrance
6. North Court

*In 1924, a life-size statue of King Zoser was discovered at Saqqara by Cecil Firth. Wearing a Sed cloak, worn by the king during his jubilee Sed festival, the statue would have been given offerings on behalf of the dead king.*

## KING ZOSER'S BURIAL CHAMBER

The burial chamber was located underneath the Step Pyramid, surrounded by a maze of passages decorated with carvings and hieroglyphs recording the king's name.

## Lesson 4
# The Great Pyramids

The magnificent pyramids of Giza are the most famous of all Ancient Egyptian monuments. Each pyramid was part of a larger burial complex that included a valley temple, to which the king's body was brought by boat; a connecting causeway, along which the funeral procession would bring the body; and a mortuary temple for the burial ceremonies.

THE PYRAMIDS OF GIZA IN CROSS SECTION.
The pyramids of Khufu, Khaefra and Menkaura were broken into by tomb robbers long ago. Apart from the stone sarcophagi found inside, they are all now empty. They were built from limestone, with granite burial chambers and fine limestone outer casings.

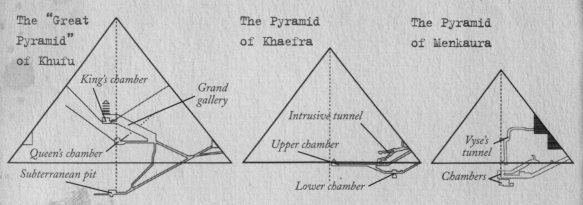

The "Great Pyramid" of Khufu
King's chamber
Grand gallery
Queen's chamber
Subterranean pit

The Pyramid of Khaefra
Intrusive tunnel
Upper chamber
Lower chamber

The Pyramid of Menkaura
Vyse's tunnel
Chambers

*With their fine white limestone outer casings, the pyramids must have looked even more magnificent in antiquity. Sadly, most of the outer casings were removed and used to rebuild the city of Cairo after an earthquake.*

# HOW WERE THE PYRAMIDS BUILT?

No one is sure how the great pyramids were built. More than two million blocks were used for the Great Pyramid alone, each one weighing about two and a half tons. Here are three theories, each with its own advantages and drawbacks.

## THEORY 1: Earth Ramps

Stones would have been dragged up huge ramps of earth and put in place. But such ramps would need vast amounts of earth to build.

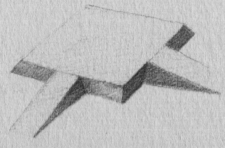

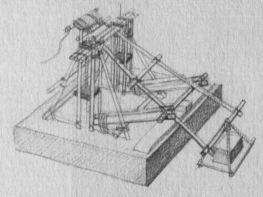

## THEORY 2: Pulleys and Cranes

Enormous pulleys are built to hoist each stone into place. But these pulleys would need to be incredibly strong and tall to reach the top of the pyramid.

## THEORY 3: Spiral Causeway

Pathways of mud brick would have been coiled around the edge of the pyramid and the stones pulled up on sledges. But no evidence of mud brick pathways has been found.

ACTIVITY: There are some very strange theories as to how the pyramids were built. What is the strangest theory you can find?

# *The Middle Kingdom: 2040 to 1750 BC*

At the end of the Old Kingdom, Ancient Egypt entered a time now known as the First Intermediate Period. The ordered life of the Old Kingdom was swept away as tradition and central government under a single king broke down. When order was eventually re-established by the Pharaohs of the Middle Kingdom, Ancient Egyptian society had begun to look a little different.

*The Middle Kingdom kings came from Thebes and brought their local god, Amun (pictured below), with them when they rose to power. Soon he was worshipped throughout Egypt as king of the gods.*

*Although the kings were still seen as godlike, ordinary people had begun to enjoy more privilege and the wealthy also began to create lavish tombs. This painting above shows one of those tombs at Beni Hasan, cut into the face of the rock.*

## TOMB RAIDERS

To achieve safe passage to the afterlife, it was essential that the mummified body and its precious belongings remain undisturbed. Tomb builders devised many clever defences against tomb robbers, such as false doors and secret passageways, but sadly many of them failed. So many tombs now being excavated lie empty, with only a few tantalising fragments left behind.

ACTIVITY: After an archaeological dig, you discover that the labels have come off your valuable finds. Can you correctly identify these objects and give each one the right label?

1.

2.

3.

4.

A. A brain hook was used to remove the brain before mummification.

B. Canopic jars were used to store the internal organs of the deceased.

C. A throw stick was a weapon that was used for hunting birds.

D. This bracelet once belonged to an Egyptian queen called Ahotep.

ANSWERS: 1—B; 2—A; 3—D; 4—C

19

# Pyramid Texts and Tombs

The Ancient Egyptians believed that writing contained great power. From the time of the Pharaoh Unas at the end of the Old Kingdom, and right through the Middle Kingdom, the walls of the royal burial chambers were covered in hieroglyphs. These Pyramid Texts were spells and magical incantations to be used by the dead king to help him in his journey to the afterlife.

*Many tombs show their occupant's name repeated over and over, in the belief that if a dead person's name was spoken, they would live again. Can you find the name Pepi repeated four times in this fragment from his tomb?*

= P P
= I I

## COFFIN TEXTS

During the Middle Kingdom, rich people were buried in wooden coffins, decorated with brightly coloured writing. Like the royal pyramid texts, these coffin texts contained potent magic to protect the dead person and ensure their wellbeing in the afterlife.

*Ancient Egyptian Coffin*

## THE AFTERLIFE

Ancient Egyptians believed that what was shown on the walls of their tombs would also exist in the afterlife. They were careful to depict whatever they required for a comfortable existence after death, whether it was food, servants or music to last for eternity, either as paintings or as models.

ACTIVITY: These pictures come from the tomb walls of a rich Egyptian named Ti, Overseer of Royal Mortuary Structures. Which activities did he wish to enjoy in the afterlife?

1.

2.

3.

Draw some tomb pictures of your own life. You could even try adding your name in hieroglyphs (See pages 50-51 for help).

ANSWERS 1. Building Boats 2. Hunting Hippos 3. Herding cranes.

# Lesson 7
## An Ancient Egyptian Tale

This Middle Kingdom tale, THE STORY OF THE SHIPWRECKED SAILOR, was written by Amenaa, son of Ameny, the cunning-fingered scribe, may he live long in health and wealth.

I was on my way to the Pharaoh's mines on a fine ship, in the company of one hundred and fifty of Egypt's best sailors. As we approached land, the winds picked up and the waves grew high and soon our ship was lost. I managed to seize a piece of wood to save myself, but all the other sailors were drowned.

The waves washed me ashore on a deserted island, but luckily I found plenty of food — figs, melons, fish and fowl — and I lacked for nothing. And so I lit a fire and made an offering to the gods. All of a sudden there was a noise like thunder; the trees shook and the ground trembled and I saw a huge serpent!

It was mighty, blue as lapis lazuli and all overlaid with gold. It drew itself up before me as I cowered on the ground, and three times it asked me, "What has brought you here, little one? If you don't tell me, I will make you vanish just like a flame." And it carried me away in its mouth.

I told the serpent about my voyage and the shipwreck. And it said to me, "Fear not. If you have come to me, it is God who let you live and brought you here to this blessed isle." And it said that I would remain on its island for four months, until a ship came bearing sailors from my own land to take me home to my wife and children.

The serpent seemed to enjoy company and conversation, and it talked at length with me. It told me how it lived on the island of plenty with its kindred, and how there were 75 serpents altogether.

I bowed and told it that it would be rewarded by the Pharaoh, with gifts of perfume, oil and ships laden with treasures. But it just smiled and said, "I am the Prince of Punt and I already have such riches. When you depart from my island, you will never see it again, for it will be changed into waves."

Time went by, and, just as the serpent had said, after four months had passed, one day I saw a ship. I climbed up a tree so I could see who was aboard, and then rushed to tell the serpent. It already knew all about it, and said, "Farewell, farewell. Go home, little one. Within two months you will be at your house once more. Embrace your children and may your name be blessed amongst your people."

I bowed and thanked the serpent, and it gave me parting gifts of perfume, sweet wood, kohl, incense and ivory. I went down to the shore and met the sailors who took me aboard their ship.

Just as the serpent had said, after two months we arrived home again, and I sought out the Pharaoh's courtiers and before the whole court I presented the Pharaoh with the serpent's gifts and my story was heard.

ACTIVITY: This is one of the most famous Ancient Egyptian tales. Another is THE STORY OF SINUHE. See if you can find it in your local library.

After the Middle Kingdom, Egypt was ruled by foreigners, known as the Hyksos kings who introduced the horse, the chariot and new bronze weapons. These weapons would prove very useful to the warrior-kings who dominated the New Kingdom. These kings were determined to make Egypt as strong as possible and waged war against their neighbours, creating the most powerful empire of the ancient world.

*Rameses II in his war chariot*

THE FEMALE PHARAOH

Not all of the New Kingdom kings were warlike. When Pharaoh Thutmosis II died, his widow, Hatshepsut, acted first as regent for her nephew Thutmosis III and for 15 years ruled as Pharaoh alone.

*Hatshepsut's mortuary temple, built into the rock near the Valley of the Kings, is still an impressive sight.*

*Hatshepsut, above, wasn't the only female Pharaoh, but all adopted the symbolic artificial beard of the Pharaoh.*

## AFTER THE NEW KINGDOM — ALEXANDER

When the New Kingdom ended, Ancient Egypt again fell under the sway of foreign rulers. The Persians, who ruled Egypt until 332 BC, were so unpopular that when Alexander the Great defeated them, he was greeted as a liberator by the Ancient Egyptian people. He founded the city of Alexandria, which became renowned as a centre of culture and learning based around its famous museum and library.

*A coin bearing the image of Alexander the Great*

*The Temple of Horus at Edfu was rebuilt by Alexander's successor, Ptolemy I, who founded a new dynasty of Greek Pharaohs.*

## CLEOPATRA

Queen Cleopatra VII is one of the most famous figures in Ancient Egyptian history. She inherited the throne at a time when the Roman Empire was closing in on Egypt. Intelligent and ambitious, she had affairs with both Julius Caesar and Mark Antony. After Antony's defeat, she is said to have killed herself rather than be humiliated by Rome. Her death marks the end of Ancient Egypt.

*An image of Queen Cleopatra.*

ACTIVITY: Design a coin commemorating Cleopatra's reign, with her head on one side and an event from her life on the other.

# The Valley of the Kings

The tombs of the New Kingdom Pharaohs lie across the Nile from Luxor, in the Valley of the Kings. Most of these tombs were plundered in antiquity, their treasures taken and the royal mummies reburied in groups. But Howard Carter, the famous Egyptologist, was convinced that one tomb had escaped discovery. He spent years searching and digging until, in 1922, he finally uncovered a mysterious flight of stone steps leading to a tomb entrance.

This solid gold mummy mask is made in the image of King Tutankhamen

*Making a hole in the tomb door, Carter looked into the antechamber. He was amazed to see that the contents were almost intact and that there were "animals, statues, and gold — everywhere the glint of gold."*

26

## INSIDE THE TOMB

The contents of Tutankhamen's tomb told a story: Long ago, robbers had begun a raid but were interrupted, scattering treasures on the floor as they escaped. All was jumbled together: linen, jewel boxes, gold rings and perfumes. But at the heart of the tomb, in his burial chamber, King Tutankhamen lay undisturbed in his cocoon of three coffins.

Tutankhamen's outer two coffins were plated in gold.

The inner coffin was made of 240 pounds of solid gold.

A 'Mummy's Curse' is said to protect the tombs of the Pharaohs. Lord Carnarvon's death shortly after the opening of Tutankhamen's tomb was supposedly evidence of this curse in action. But as I write this in 1926 at least, Howard Carter and his assistants seem to have escaped it...

1. Entrance tunnel
2. Antechamber
3. Annexe
4. Burial chamber
5. Treasury

ACTIVITY: Place these three objects in the room in the tomb where Howard Carter discovered them.

Cow-bed

Treasury guardian

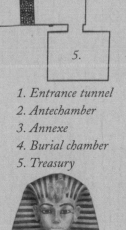

Mummy mask

ANSWER: Treasury guardian, treasury; Cow-bed, antechamber; Mummy mask, burial chamber.

N
NW | NE
W ——— E
SW | SE
S

Natron

Cultivated
Land

✠ MEMPHIS

Copper

Limestone

Siwa
Oasis

Bahariya
Oasis

Alabaster

Farafra
Oasis

Limestone

Schist

Dahkla
Oasis

El-Kharga
Oasis

✠ THEBES

Gold

This map shows some of the resources of
Ancient Egypt. Ancient Egyptians
also imported many things: wood from
Lebanon, ivory from Assyria, olive oil
from Crete and incense from Punt.

Sandstone

Amethyst

✠ ASWAN

Granite

Copper

Gold

# Part II.
## Life and Culture in Ancient Egypt

*The gentle man overcomes all obstacles.*
*He who makes himself work all day will*
*never know a moment of enjoyment, but he*
*who spends all day enjoying himself will*
*not be able to hold on to his wealth.*
*"The Wisdom of Ptah-hotep", c1900 BC*

The history of Ancient Egypt is not merely the history of kings and queens. For many thousands of years, the culture that grew up along the banks of the Nile was one of the most civilised in the Ancient World. Ancient Egypt was rich in resources and those that it lacked, such as wood or olive oil, it was able to import from its neighbours. This allowed civilised culture to develop.

In some villages that have been excavated, such as Deir El Medina on the West Bank at Luxor, there is evidence that a large number of the population could read and write, including a number of women.

# Lesson 10
## Life on the Flooding Nile

The rhythms of the river Nile defined many aspects of Ancient Egyptian life. Every year the river had a season of flooding, when the water would rise to cover the farm land. When it receded once more, the fields would be left covered in a layer of fertile, black silt. But if the Nile rose too high, it might cause damage, sweeping away people's homes. And if the water levels weren't high enough, the whole country would suffer from the famine that resulted from a bad harvest.

The Ancient Egyptians called Egypt 'Kemet', or the 'black land', while the vast desert area that lay beyond the black fertile strip was called 'Desheret,' or the 'Red land'.

The god of the flooding Nile is Hapi, shown here. His plump appearance represents the plentiful bounty of the river.

THE "BENNU BIRD"
The Ancient Egyptians were great boat-builders. Our hired sailing barge — or "dahabeeyah" — the "Bennu Bird" is the modern descendant of those ancient boats.

*Much mythology is tied up with the Nile. This scene, right, from the walls of the temple at Edfu shows Horus fighting his enemy Seth, who has taken on the form of a hippo*

ACTIVITY: The Ancient Egyptians would undertake some tasks when the river was in flood and others when the flood had receded. Decide which of these activities are best done when the Nile is in flood and which when it is out of flood.

*Building pyramids*

*Planting seeds*

*Harvesting crops*

*Going to war*

ANSWER: It is best to build pyramids and go to war during the flood season, as you cannot farm the land then, but planting and harvesting crops must be done before the flood returns.

# Eat Like an Egyptian

Rich Ancient Egyptians loved to
entertain and would have served up
feasts including such delicacies
as pigeon stew, roast quail,
spiced honey cakes and fresh
berries. Although not everyone
could eat as well as this, it
is certain that many people would
have enjoyed a wide variety of
foods such as meat, fish, eggs,
cheese, grapes, figs, melons,
onions, garlic, leeks and lettuce.

*Making
bread*

### DAILY BREAD

For ordinary Ancient Egyptians,
bread was the most important
food. Sometimes workers were
paid in grain. Grinding the
barley or emmer wheat to make
each day's flour was a hard job
usually done by women.

### EASY FISH

The Nile was full of fish, and
when the flood receded, some
were left high and dry on the
banks. They could be grilled
straightaway or preserved by
drying or pickling in salt.

## HUNTING FOR FOOD

While some Pharaohs enjoyed elephant-hunting expeditions, it was more common to hunt animals that could be eaten, such as hares, antelope, gazelles and different kinds of waterfowl and birds.

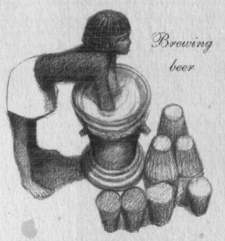

*Brewing beer*

## BEER

Most Ancient Egyptians drank beer. This was because beer was often healthier to drink than unclean water from the Nile, which might well have carried disease. Wine was also available for rich people.

ACTIVITY: Try making this Ancient Egyptian recipe.

### HUMMUS
300g/12oz cooked chickpeas
juice of 1 lemon
2 cloves garlic
sesame seed oil
1/2 tsp salt

Mash up the cooked chickpeas, then add the lemon juice, chopped garlic and as much sesame seed oil as it takes to make a paste smooth enough to spread on bread. This tasty dish is as popular today as it was thousands of years ago.

# Dress Like an Egyptian

Ancient Egyptians took great care with their appearance. Most clothing was made of linen, and varied from simple shifts to richly decorated, pleated robes. Wealthy people shaved their heads and wore elaborately styled wigs to protect them from the hot sun and guard against lice. Children had a hairstyle that would seem strange to us today: both boys and girls had their hair shaved off, except for a lock hanging down by the ear.

Ancient Egyptians used perfumed oils to clean, protect and scent their skin. A jar of perfumed oil was found in the tomb of Tutankhamun as part of his equipment for the afterlife.

At parties and special occasions, a host might offer guests perfumed cones of wax to place on their heads. As they heated up, the cones would melt and slowly drip down the guests' hair and faces!

## MAKE UP

Both men and women wore eye make-up known as kohl, which also protected against the strong glare of the sun. It was ground to a paste on a palette and then carefully applied with the help of a mirror.

## JEWELLERY

The Ancient Egyptians loved jewellery. Metals and stones such as gold, lapis lazuli, amethyst, turquoise and precious gems were worked into exquisite bracelets, ear-rings, necklaces and rings.

*Left: A statue of Queen Nefertiti*
*Below: Bracelets of King Djer*

ACTIVITY: Working at a dig, you've uncovered these objects. What are they?

1.

2.

3.

4.

ANSWERS: 1. a comb, 2. a mirror, 3. perfume jars, 4. a bracelet

# An Egyptian Village

When the New Kingdom kings began building tombs in the Valley of the Kings, they needed workmen nearby. A village of craftspeople was set up at Deir el-Medina. When excavated, it gave fascinating insights into the lives of ordinary Egyptians. Remains of letters and lists written by the workers were found there. Reading over these fragments — from laundry lists to evidence in court cases — we can catch glimpses of the concerns of real people thousands of years ago.

A HOUSE PLAN

Deir el-Medina was surrounded by a wall, with one entrance to the north. There was a main street and about 70 narrow houses, all constructed to a similar design.

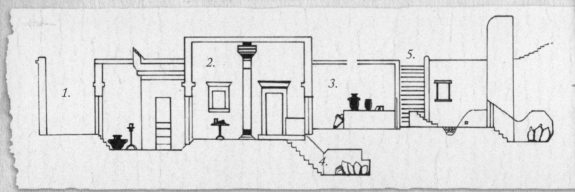

1. *Entrance hall*
2. *Main room*
3. *Kitchen*
4. *Storage room or cellar*
5. *Stairs to open roof area*

*This plan shows the cross-section of a typical house in Deir el-Medina. These houses were designed to stay as cool as possible.*

## LETTERS FROM DEIR EL-MEDINA

The people living at Deir el-Medina were highly skilled and included carpenters, sculptors and coppersmiths as well as doctors, scribes and the officials who oversaw the workers. Scholars disagree as to how many of these people could write themselves and how many would have asked scribes to write for them. People wrote on papyrus and also on thin limestone pieces called ostraca.

ACTIVITY: When these ostraca were first excavated, some had fallen to pieces and had to be reconstructed. Here we have translated some of them. Can you fit the pieces together?

*A.*

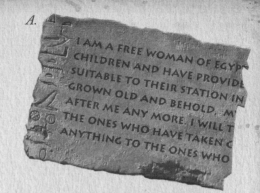

I AM A FREE WOMAN OF EGYP
CHILDREN AND HAVE PROVIDE
SUITABLE TO THEIR STATION IN
GROWN OLD AND BEHOLD, M
AFTER ME ANY MORE. I WILL T
THE ONES WHO HAVE TAKEN C
ANYTHING TO THE ONES WHO

*B.*

MENTMOSE PROMISED HIM
BARLEY FROM MY BROTHER.
THIS TRANSACTION. MAY R
ON THAT DAY THE WORKMA
FRESH FAT TO THE CHIEF OF

*C.*

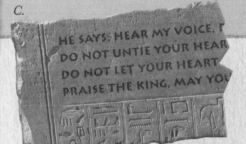

HE SAYS: HEAR MY VOICE,
DO NOT UNTIE YOUR HEAR
DO NOT LET YOUR HEART
PRAISE THE KING. MAY YO

*E.*

I WILL PAY YOU FOR IT WITH
MY BROTHER WILL GUARANTEE
E KEEP YOU IN GOOD HEALTH.
N MENNA GAVE A POT OF
POLICE MENTMOSE.

*D.*

. I HAVE RAISED EIGHT
D THEM WITH EVERYTHING
LIFE. BUT NOW I HAVE
CHILDREN DON'T LOOK
HEREFORE GIVE MY GOODS TO
ARE OF ME. I WILL NOT GIVE
HAVE NEGLECTED ME.

*F.*

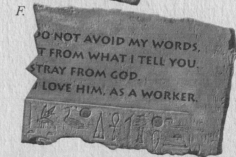

DO NOT AVOID MY WORDS,
T FROM WHAT I TELL YOU.
STRAY FROM GOD.
LOVE HIM, AS A WORKER.

ANSWERS: A & D, from "The Will of Lady Naunakhte."
B & E, from "The Trial of Mentmose."
C & F, from "The Teaching Made by a Man for his Son."

# Jobs and Work in Ancient Egypt

Many jobs in Ancient Egypt would have been similar to ones we
know today. People worked as farmers, soldiers, midwives,
butchers, carpenters and so on. Other professions were linked to
Ancient Egypt's particular traditions – embalmers and temple
priests – or were connected to the government or king, like the
vizier, the palace dancers and the Pharaoh's royal fan-bearer.

*Anubis was the patron god
of embalmers and healers.*

ACTIVITY: Decide what these people did from
the translations of their tomb inscriptions:

**B.**
ONE WHO UNDERSTANDS THE INTERNAL
FLUIDS AND WHO IS GUARDIAN OF THE BODY.
CURE FOR INDIGESTION:
CRUSH A BOAR'S TOOTH AND PUT IT INSIDE
FOUR HONEY CAKES. EAT FOR FOUR DAYS.

**A.**
I KNOW THE SECRETS OF THE
HIEROGLYPHS AND HOW TO MIX
PIGMENTS. BECAUSE I AM AN
EXCELLENT CRAFTSMAN, I KNOW
HOW TO CREATE THE POSTURE OF
A MAN'S STATUE AND FORM THE
GRACE OF A WOMAN'S STATUE,
HOW TO SHOW BIRDS IN FLIGHT
OR THE SPEED OF THE RUNNER.

**C.**
HIS MAJESTY COMMANDED MY WEAPONS
TRAINING, TOGETHER WITH SIX MEN OF HIS
PALACE... IN BATTLE I GUARDED THE REAR OF
THE ARMY AND WHEN WE FOUGHT AGAINST
THE ASIATICS, I ATTACKED AND NEVER CEASED
FROM THE FIGHT. BLESS MY EYES, I NEVER RAN
AWAY. HIS MAJESTY REWARDED ME HIMSELF
AND GAVE ME A THROW-STICK, A DAGGER
AND A SHEATH ALL WORKED IN GOLD.

ANSWERS: A. The Draughtsman Irtysen;
B. The Doctor; C. The Soldier.

MYTH: The Egyptians used thousands of slaves to build their monuments.
FACT: Slavery was rare in Ancient Egypt. However, there was a system where ordinary people owed a certain portion of their working life to the Pharaoh, a bit like military service.

MYTH: Women didn't work outside the home.
FACT: Although many women did devote themselves to running their household and the task of bearing children, as we have seen, some women occupied the most prestigious and responsible positions in Egypt, including that of Pharaoh.

MYTH: Workers were paid in gold.
FACT: There was no equivalent of our currency in Ancient Egypt. A barter system was used in which goods like grain, oil, cattle or copper were valued against each other. For example, one pig might be worth five copper rings.

MYTH: The workers were driven very hard and had no holidays.
FACT: Records show people at Deir el-Medina had two days off after eight days of work, and a working day was eight hours long with a lunch break. Records also show that they sometimes went on strike.

# Fun and Games in Ancient Egypt

Archaeological evidence shows that the Ancient Egyptians really knew how to live the good life. Not only did they love feasting, music and dancing, but they also enjoyed a whole range of games and sport. Everyone, from the royal family to the poorest peasant, would have played the popular board games Dogs and Jackals (a bit like Snakes and Ladders) and Senet, although not everyone would own an inlaid ebony and ivory playing board like Tutankhamen's!

*Senet was a game for two players, a bit like our game of backgammon. The aim was to move pieces round the board to the last five squares and then remove them.*

Children would have played many different games — some of which are still familiar like marbles or catch. In one game, you tried to jump over the linked arms of your opponents, in another you played catch sitting on the back of a team-mate.

Young children might have played with a doll made of rags and papyrus, or a toy animal made of wood with moving parts, like this cat.

It is likely that children loved listening to stories. Some people believe this papyrus from Thebes could be the first ever children's book.

ACTIVITY: Find your way through the marshes to hunt ducks. You mustn't go down a channel that ends in a crocodile or hippo, and watch out for your vizier, who is hiding to make sure you have an "accident" so he can replace you as Pharaoh. Answer on p43.

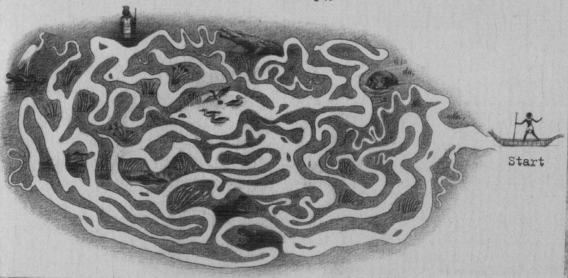

Start

## Lesson 16
# Travel and Trade in Ancient Egypt

The Ancient Egyptians didn't enjoy travel, partly because they believed that Egypt was the best land in the whole world, and partly because if they died abroad they would not be able to receive a proper Egyptian burial. However, although Egypt was a wealthy country it lacked some necessities, and expeditions were organised to exchange Egypt's gold, grain and other goods for wood, precious stones, spices, incense, silver and tin.

THE EXPEDITION TO PUNT
The Pharaoh Hatshepsut ordered an expedition to an African land known as Punt, which might have been on the Red Sea coast. It was rich in the incense, perfumes and resins needed for temple ritual and mummification.

Hatshepsut was so proud of her expedition that she commissioned pictures of it to be added to the walls of her mortuary temple at Deir El Bahri. The sketches you see here, however, are copies of sketches made around one hundred years ago, for now the colouring is almost too faded to see.

ACTIVITY: Imagine you are travelling to Punt to buy 6 animal skins for your priests, 20 incense trees and 35 precious gems. Work out how many Egyptian goods — such as honey, grain, gold and cloth — you might need to take with you to Punt.

Goods from Egypt

1 gold ring
1/2 sack grain
30 jars honey
10 linen shirts

} is worth {

Goods from Punt

4 incense trees
3 leopard skins
7 precious stones

SUGGESTED ANSWER: You could take 2 gold rings to exchange for the 6 leopard skins, 2 1/2 sacks of grain to exchange for the incense trees and 50 linen shirts to exchange for the 35 precious stones.

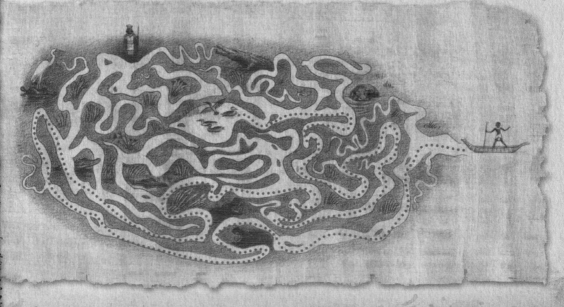

# Lesson 17
## Palace Life

Today we know more about Ancient Egyptian tombs than we know about their palaces because the palaces were largely made of mudbrick and were not built to last for eternity. Excavations show that the king's vast palaces provided a luxurious home for the king and his family. They were also the centre of government and the base for the king's court, his vizier and all the nobles who surrounded the king in the hope of gaining royal favour.

*The royal family, Pharaoh Akhenaten, Queen Nefertiti and their daughters, distribute 'gold of honour' to royal favourites from the Window of Appearances in their palace at Akhetaten.*

### RUNNING THE PALACE

Maintaining the highest standards of comfort and luxury was a full-time job for the workers in the palace kitchens, storerooms, workshops and offices. The Pharaoh must have had hundreds or even thousands of servants, each with his or her own particular duties to ensure the smooth running of the enormous royal household!

ACTIVITY: Look at this overhead view of the royal palace of King Akhenaten. Can you label the following rooms on the plan: royal bedroom, treasure chamber, shrine, and throne room?

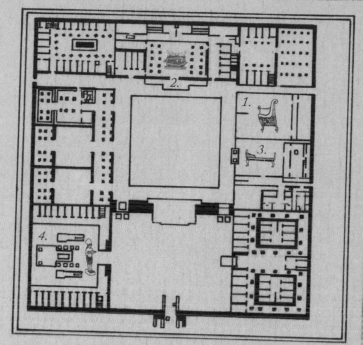

## PALACE RICHES

The Pharaoh was also the wealthiest person in Ancient Egypt, and his royal treasury would have been overflowing with riches — produce from his land, taxes and tribute sent from foreign rulers. Sometimes the gifts from overseas included exotic animals for the king's personal botanical gardens and zoo!

Although the Ancient Egyptians of the Old and Middle Kingdoms did go to war, it wasn't until the New Kingdom that Egypt became an advanced military power. By this time, the army had more sophisticated weapons, including the wheeled chariot and a composite bow. The army itself was made up of a mixture of conscripts, professional Egyptian soldiers and foreign mercenaries, all under the command of a general who in turn answered to the Pharaoh himself.

*Rameses II in his war chariot*

## THE MAKEUP OF THE ARMY
The army of Rameses II was divided into four divisions of 5,000 men. These were divided in turn into 20 companies of 250 men. Finally there were five smaller groups of 50 soldiers each of whom answered to their captain, the "greatest of fifty".

*This scene, from Rameses II's Temple at Abu Simbel, shows the king single-handedly charging the enemy at the Battle of Kadesh. This battle led to a peace treaty between the Hittites and the Ancient Egyptians.*

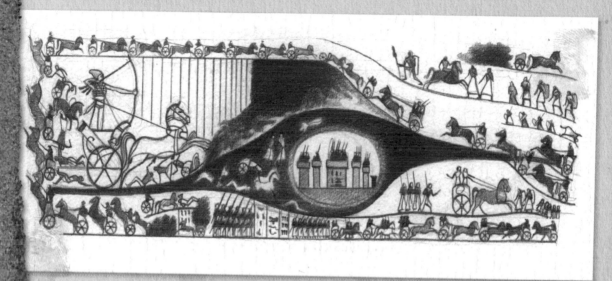

ACTIVITY: Identify these common Egyptian weapons of the New and Middle Kingdoms. Choose from: Axe, Spear, Dagger, Throw stick, Khepesh Sword, Bow and Arrow.

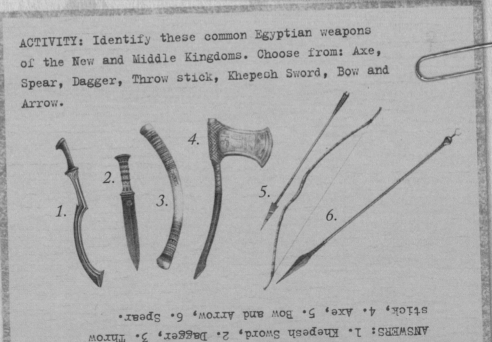

ANSWERS: 1. Khepesh Sword, 2. Dagger, 3. Throw stick, 4. Axe, 5. Bow and Arrow, 6. Spear.

# Reading Hieroglyphs

The meaning of hieroglyphs, the Ancient Egyptian sacred writings used by the priests and scribes, was unknown until the signs were deciphered in the nineteenth century, thanks to the discovery of an essential key by French soldiers: a block of carved granite which came to be called the Rosetta Stone. It was written in two languages — Ancient Greek and Egyptian, and in three scripts — Ancient Greek, Demotic, the common script of Ancient Egypt, and Hieroglyphic, the sacred script.

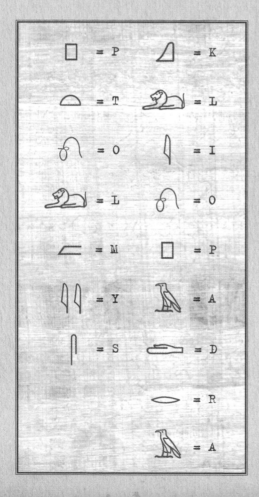

CHAMPOLLION

**The man who finally deciphered the Rosetta Stone was called Jean François Champollion. He realised that most hieroglyphs stood for sounds, which he transliterated into the letters of our alphabet that represented roughly similar sounds. He also learned that special names — such as the names of Pharaohs — might be recorded in ovals called "cartouches". By comparing the three texts on the Rosetta Stone, and also by comparing two names on the stone to the same names on an obelisk from Philae, he was first able to identify two royal names — Ptolemy and Cleopatra.**

| | | | | | | |
|---|---|---|---|---|---|---|
| = I | = MN | = N | = MR | = RA | = MS | = SS |

*Above, this picture shows the name Rameses-meryamun, one of the names of Rameses II, the king who built Abu Simbel. As was usual, the name of the god Amun is written first, although it is pronounced last.*

ACTIVITY: Translate these names of 19th Dynasty Pharaohs.

Note: you will find all the signs you need to help you on the next page.

□ = PR

= AA

*Right, the king of Egypt came to be called Pharaoh by the Greeks, from the title Per Aa meaning 'Great House'.*

# Writing Hieroglyphs

Ancient Egyptian hieroglyphs are made up of picture symbols.
Most symbols stood for sounds, and could be combined with other
symbols to make up a word. For example, the symbol ⌒ (r) and
the symbol ∿ (n) could both be combined together to make the
word ⌒∿ (rn) meaning 'name'. We don't know how the Ancient
Egyptians pronounced this word, so we add an 'e' between the
letters to make it easier to say as 'ren'.

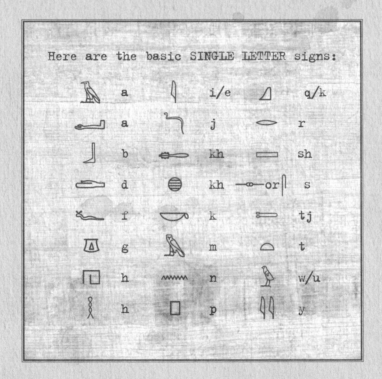

Here are the basic SINGLE LETTER signs:

| | | | | | |
|---|---|---|---|---|---|
| 𓄿 | a | | i/e | | q/k |
| | a | | j | ⌒ | r |
| | b | | kh | | sh |
| | d | | kh | —∘—or | s |
| | f | | k | | tj |
| | g | | m | | t |
| | h | ∿ | n | | w/u |
| | h | | p | | y |

As well as these single-letter hieroglyphs, we have some
hieroglyphs which represent more than one letter, for example the
symbols ☐ (pr), ⌡ (nfr) and ☥ (ankh). Again, we add an 'e' to
the first two so we can pronounce them as 'per' and 'nefer'.

Here are some signs made up of TWO or THREE sylables:

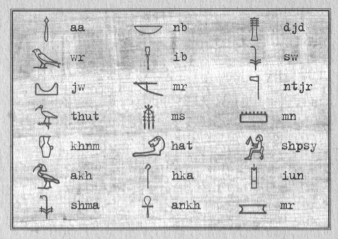

| | | | | | |
|---|---|---|---|---|---|
| | aa | | nb | | djd |
| | wr | | ib | | sw |
| | jw | | mr | | ntjr |
| | thut | | ms | | mn |
| | khnm | | hat | | shpsy |
| | akh | | hka | | iun |
| | shma | | ankh | | mr |

So far, we have learnt that Egyptian hieroglyphs represent sounds, or sound combinations, which are put together to make words, just like the letters in our own alphabet. However, there is another kind of symbol used by the Ancient Egyptians, called a 'determinative'. These symbols represented a thing or an idea, and were usually put at the end of a word to show what kind of word it was. For example, ⊗ in a word meant that the word was the name of a town or a place, while △ stood for motion.  Here are the names of two towns: Djedu (Busiris) and Abdju (Abydos).

Here are some DETERMINATIVE signs:

| | | | | | | | |
|---|---|---|---|---|---|---|---|
| | man | | woman | | motion | | weak, small |
| | god | | sun, Ra | | plural | | abstract idea |

ANSWERS TO PHARAOH HIEROGLYPHS

1. Thutmosis (Tht-Ms-S)

2. Khenmetamun-Hatshepsut(Khnm-T-I-Mn-N Hat-Shpsy)

3. Akhenaten (Akh-kh-N-I-T-N + "sun" symbol)

4. Tutankhamen-hekaiunushema (T-U-T-ANKH-I-Mn-N Hka-Iun-Shma)

5. Rameses-meryamun (Ra-Ms-S-Sw Mr-I-Mn-N)

Remember Ptah, Aten and Amun are usually written first!

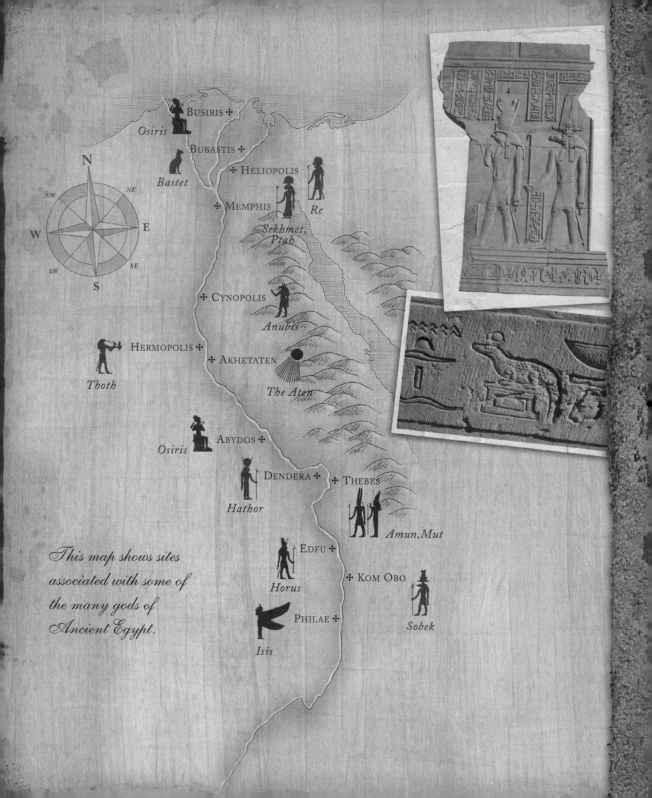

N
NW · NE
W · E
SW · SE
S

BUSIRIS ✟
*Osiris*
BUBASTIS ✟
*Bastet*
✟ HELIOPOLIS
✟ MEMPHIS
*Re*
*Sekhmet, Ptah*

HERMOPOLIS ✟
*Thoth*

✟ CYNOPOLIS
*Anubis*

✟ AKHETATEN
*The Aten*

ABYDOS ✟
*Osiris*

DENDERA ✟
✟ THEBES
*Hathor*
*Amun, Mut*

EDFU ✟
*Horus*
✟ KOM OBO

PHILAE ✟
*Isis*
*Sobek*

*This map shows sites*
*associated with some of*
*the many gods of*
*Ancient Egypt.*

# Part III

# Gods and Religion in Ancient Egypt

The Ancient Egyptians believed in many gods, and many different kinds of gods. There were national gods, such as Amun, Mut, Ptah and Re, and there were also local gods linked to one's own town or city. There were gods associated with certain beasts, such as Sobek, the crocodile god. And there were also gods associated with certain jobs, such as Anubis, god of embalmers, and gods associated with certain aspects of life and death, such as Osiris, the lord of the underworld. Having so many gods meant that Ancient Egypt was a land full of temples, and one where there were many festivals and celebrations!

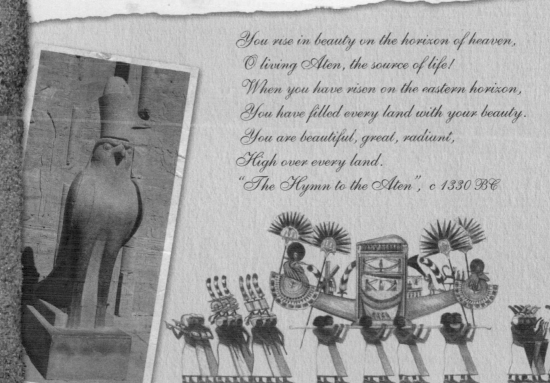

*You rise in beauty on the horizon of heaven,*
*O living Aten, the source of life!*
*When you have risen on the eastern horizon,*
*You have filled every land with your beauty.*
*You are beautiful, great, radiant,*
*High over every land.*
*"The Hymn to the Aten", c 1330 BC*

# The Many Gods of Ancient Egypt

The Ancient Egyptians worshipped many different gods. However, an ordinary Egyptian wouldn't have prayed to all these gods at once. Instead, there might have been a local god or 'family' of gods who were the main focus of worship. Other gods would have been asked for help at specific times, for example, the goddess Taweret was seen as the protector of women during childbirth, Bes, the protector of the home, while Osiris, left, was lord of the afterlife.

*The Ancient Egyptians built many temples, such as this one at Philae — seen before it was engulfed by the waters held back by the 1902 Aswan dam.*

ACTIVITY: Ancient Egyptian gods often came in "triads" of three gods - a father, a mother, and a child. Can you match each god to the correct description for the triad below?

1.        2.        3.

Amun was worshipped at Thebes as 'king of the gods'. Mut, a mother goddess, was sometimes shown as a vulture. Khonsu, the moon god, had a child's side-lock of hair.

ANSWERS: 1. Khonsu, 2. Amun, 3. Mut

## ISIS AND OSIRIS

Ancient Egyptians believed that Egypt was once ruled by Osiris and his wife and sister Isis. However, their jealous brother Seth killed Osiris, hiding parts of his body in different places.

**ISIS**

**OSIRIS**

*Transforming herself into a kite, Isis collected the parts of her dead husband's body and breathed life back into them. She is called the mistress of magic.*

*Osiris, the murdered king, became lord of the underworld after his death. He is often shown with green skin that represents rebirth and regeneration.*

**HORUS**

**SETH**

*Hawk-headed Horus was the son of Isis and Osiris. He began a long battle with Seth, finally defeating him to become king of Egypt. Later kings identified themselves as Horus.*

*Seth was the god of the desert and of storms. As the murderer of Osiris, he was both feared for his brutal ferocity and yet admired for his strength and also for his cunning.*

# *An Ancient Egyptian Myth*

This tale, THE STORY OF RE, tells of the creation of the earth, and of how the god Re grew angry with mankind and tried to destroy them using his daughter, the terrible goddess Sekhmet.

In the beginning there was the all-powerful god Re. He made the other gods: Shu – the winds that blew, Tefnut – the rain that fell, Geb – the earth, and Nut – the sky goddess. And Re also made the god Hapi – the river Nile that flowed and made Egypt fertile. Then Re made all things on earth and he also made men. Re ruled as Pharaoh for thousands of years and it was such a time of goodness and plenty that people spoke of it fondly for ever after.

But it came to pass that Re grew old and men no longer feared or obeyed him. So Re became angry, and summoned all the other gods to him. They advised him, "Send destruction upon men and turn your Eye against them."

So Re sent his Eye against them, in the form of his daughter Sekhmet, the fiercest and most terrible of all the goddesses. Like a lion rushing upon its prey, she fell upon the people of Upper and Lower Egypt and slew all those who had disobeyed her father, Re. She killed everyone she saw and rejoiced in the slaughter, delighting in the taste of blood.

The Nile itself ran red with the blood of men, and eventually Re felt sorry for the people, but even he couldn't stop Sekhmet's blood-thirsty rampage, she was so carried away with cruelty.

Re realised he would have to trick Sekhmet into stopping, so he ordered messengers to take red ochre from the isle of Elephantine, and then bring it to him in the town of Heliopolis, where the women had been brewing beer all day long at Re's command. The red ochre was mixed with the seven thousand jars of beer and then poured out over the land where Sekhmet was planning her next slaughter.

When the sun rose the next day, Sekhmet saw the ground all flooded with the red beer and, thinking it was the blood of those she had killed, she laughed with joy and drank deeply of it. She drank so much that the strength of the beer made her powerless. She could no longer slay, but instead she slept the day away and then staggered back to her father.

Re said, "You come in peace, sweet one," and from that moment onwards she became the goddess Hathor, as sweet and strong as love itself. Each new year afterwards, the priestesses of Hathor drank the beer of Heliopolis coloured with red ochre from Elephantine to celebrate her festival.

Re continued to rule, but he was growing old and losing his wisdom. None of the other gods could take his wisdom as they didn't know his secret name of power. But then Geb and Nut had children, and the younger gods and goddesses were born: Osiris, Isis, Seth and Nephthys. Isis was the wisest of these four, and she managed to trick Re into telling her his secret name of power.

From that time on, Re was Pharaoh no longer, but took his place in the heavens, travelling across the sky each day, and crossing the Underworld each night in the Boat of Re, taking with him the souls of the dead.

## Lesson 23
# Everyday Gods of Ancient Egypt

Egyptologists need to be able to recognise Ancient Egyptian gods and goddesses, even in the darkest tomb. To assist with this, they should memorise my simple chart (right) before attempting to match the gods below with their names and descriptions.

*A lion-headed goddess of vengeance, who leads the Pharaoh into battle.*

SEKHMET

*The cow-horned goddess of love, fertility, music and dance.*

HATHOR

*A powerful, crocodile-headed god of the Nile.*

SOBEK

*This ibis-headed god of wisdom is the patron of scribes.*

THOTH

*This jackal-headed god is the patron of embalmers.*

ANUBIS

*A bearded dwarf who guards the home against evil.*

BES

*A cat goddess who is protector of the home and of domestic cats.*

BASTET

## Emily Sands says:
## "Know Your Ancient Egyptian Gods."

The success of an excavation or even finding the right site may depend on your familiarity with this chart showing many of the most popular Ancient Egyptian gods.

**RA**
Sun God

**OSIRIS**
God of the Underworld

**ISIS**
Wife of Osiris

**HORUS**
Son of Osiris

**SETH**
Evil Brother of Osiris

**THOTH**
God of Scribes and Wisdom

**HATHOR**
Goddess of Music and Love

**SOBEK**
God of Crocodiles

**SEKHMET**
Goddess of Vengeance

**ANUBIS**
God of Embalmers

**BASTET**
God of Cats and the Home

**BES**
God of the Household

# An Ancient Egyptian Temple

Ancient Egyptian temples were called the "mansions of the gods". There, statues of the gods were carefully tended by priests and servants. The closest ordinary people might come was the outer temple courtyard, and only during special festivals. The temple grew progressively more sacred towards its centre. Only priests of the highest level and the king himself were allowed to approach the sanctuary, where the god's sacred shrine or "naos" was found.

## TEMPLE WORSHIP

Three times each day, the high priest attended the god, taking offerings of food, drink, perfume and flowers. He would enter the sanctuary and take the god's statue from its shrine. There, he would remove the statue's clothes and clean it, applying fresh eye-paint and dressing it in new clothing. Finally, food and drink would be presented for the god's symbolic meal. However, fish was considered an unacceptable offering.

*Above, the priests dress the statue of Horus in the temple at Edfu.*

The impressive exterior of the Temple of Horus at Edfu: you can see its main front pylons decorated with vast reliefs showing Ptolemy XII (who completed its construction) in the presence of the gods Horus and his consort Hathor.

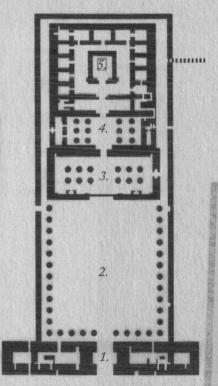

When we visited the amazingly well-preserved Temple of Horus, left, it was not difficult to imagine how imposing it must have been in its day.

1. Pylon entrance
2. Courtyard
3. Hypostyle hall
4. Antechamber
5. Naos or shrine

The Temple of Horus at Edfu

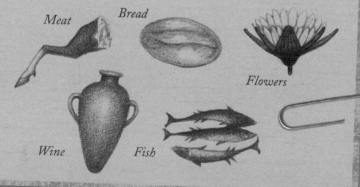

Activity: Guess which four of these things might have been among the offerings placed before Horus in the temple of Edfu.

Meat

Bread

Flowers

Wine

Fish

# Lesson 25
# Religious Festivals in Ancient Egypt

As well as the secret temple
rituals, another important part
of Ancient Egyptian religious
life was the celebration of
annual festivals. There were
over 50 festivals a year. The
Ancient Egyptians used a
calendar like ours; they used a
365-day cycle, divided into 360
days plus five sacred days
devoted to Osiris, Isis, Horus,
Seth and Nephthys.

## THE FESTIVAL OF THE BEAUTIFUL MEETING

This festival celebrated the marriage of the god Horus to
Hathor. The statue of Horus from the temple at Edfu was taken
to meet Hathor's statue - which was brought by river from
Dendera, 100 miles away. The feast included free food and drink
for all pilgrims. I'm sure it was a very popular celebration!

## THE OPET FESTIVAL

The Opet Festival honoured the gods of Karnak in a lively
celebration that renewed the Pharaoh's powers. The gods' images
were carried by boat from Karnak to the temple at Luxor. At
Luxor temple, the king withdrew with the statues for a secret
rite. The Opet Festival gave ordinary Egyptians the chance to
consult an oracle: when a statue passed, people could ask a
question. It would dip for 'yes' or back away for 'no'.

## THE SED FESTIVAL

Every thirty years, a Pharaoh had to perform the Sed Festival
(shown above) to show he was still powerful enough to rule
Egypt. How much can you find out about this festival?

## Lesson 26
# Ancient Egyptian Life After Death

By the New Kingdom, Ancient Egyptians had come to believe in the existence of an afterlife, which curiously enough was very much like Egypt. This land, where the souls of the dead enjoyed everlasting life with Osiris, its ruler, was called the Field of Reeds. It was a place of happiness and plenty, where crops grew abundantly, work was easy and life was pleasant.

TOMB BURIALS

When a mummy had been taken to its tomb, the priests carried out a ceremony called the 'Opening of the Mouth'. This enabled the dead person's ba or spirit to travel out of the body. In another part of the ceremony objects were offered that the deceased would need with them in the next life.

*These illustrations show, above. the opening of the mouth ceremony being performed on a mummy and, left, Horus leading a dead man named Ani into the presence of Osiris, the god of the afterlife.*

## THE JUDGMENT OF THE DEAD

It was believed that the dead would be judged to see if they were "true of voice". Each dead person's heart was weighed against the feather of Maat, or truth. Anubis placed it on the scales, while ibis-headed Thoth, the god of wisdom, recorded the verdict.

ACTIVITY: At the judgment of the soul, Ancient Egyptians believed they had to make what is called the 'negative confession'. This meant that they had to list a series of bad things they had NOT done while they were alive. One of the following statements is not part of the real negative confession. Be careful, if you are wrong, Thoth may release Ammat the devourer!

1. "I have not killed a man."
2. "I have borrowed the Pharaoh's favourite perfume."
3. "I have not let any man go hungry."
4. "I have not purloined the cakes of the gods."
5. "I have not taken milk from the mouths of babies."
6. "I have not driven away beasts from their pastures."

# Ancient Egyptian Mummies

In pre-dynastic times, Egyptians buried their dead in the dry sand which preserved them, often for thousands of years. But sometimes, desert animals would dig up the bodies, so they began to place the bodies in coffins. Unfortunately, bodies in coffins rot easily. Thus was born the process of protecting bodies by first embalming them, and then mummifying them.

*To prepare the body for embalming various organs were removed, including the brain, which was hooked out through the nose using a tool called a 'brain hook'.*

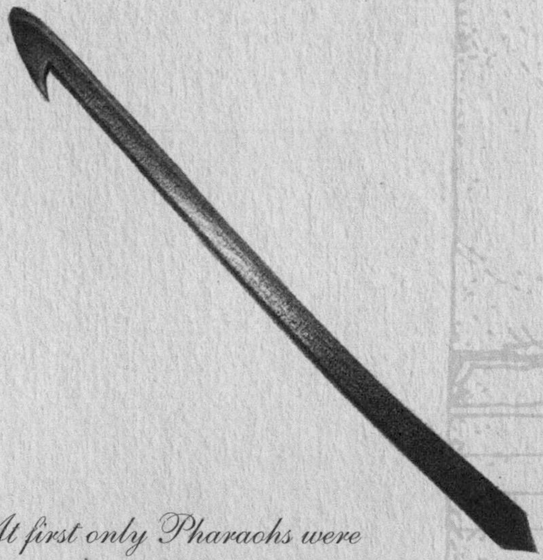

*At first only Pharaohs were mummified. This picture shows the mummy of Rameses ll. Later, the technique became available to ordinary people as well.*

## CANOPIC JARS

After the organs were removed from the body they were placed in canopic jars protected by four gods: jackal-headed Duamutef (stomach), human-headed Imsety (liver), baboon-headed Hapi (lungs), and falcon-headed Qebehsenuef (intestines).

*Imsety*

*Duamutef*

*Hapi*

*Qebehsenuef*

## THE PROCESS OF MUMMIFICATION

For Pharaohs and rich people the process usually followed these steps: Firstly, the body was washed and the organs were removed. These were preserved in canopic jars, except for the brain, which was thrown away. Secondly, the corpse was covered in a salt called natron and left to dry for 40 days. Thirdly, the body was wrapped in linen. Finally, the body was wrapped in a sheet.

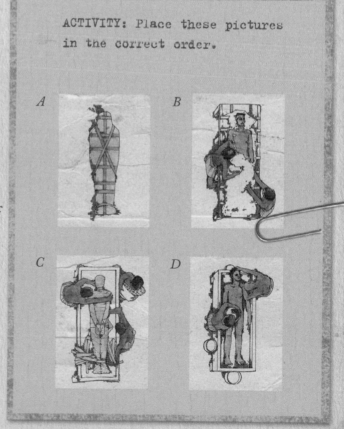

ACTIVITY: Place these pictures in the correct order.

A

B

C

D

Answer: D, B, C, A

67

# The Burial of a King

A royal burial was a vast undertaking and its organisation –
including building the tomb and creating the precious objects
to be buried alongside the mummy – might have taken decades.
Kings would have started preparations for their funerals when
they were still young. The final arrangements were made while
the body was undergoing its seventy-day mummification process.
When the mummy was ready for burial, an elaborate funeral
procession carried it to its resting place.

The king's mummy inside its golden coffin was laid on a sledge
and pulled along by oxen. Professional mourners joined the
procession, weeping, wailing, and putting dirt on their heads.
Priests were needed to carry out the appropriate rituals, burning
incense and making offerings. Items the dead person needed for the
afterlife were taken to be buried with them.

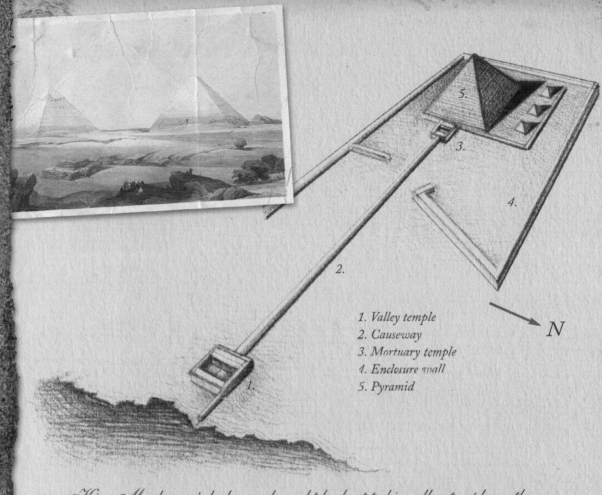

1. Valley temple
2. Causeway
3. Mortuary temple
4. Enclosure wall
5. Pyramid

King Menkaura's body was brought by boat to his valley temple on the banks of a canal cut from the Nile. Next, it was taken in procession along the covered causeway linking the valley temple to the main pyramid complex. Inside the walls of the main complex was a mortuary temple where the mummy was placed for the funeral ceremonies and where the cult of the dead king would make offerings. Finally, the mummy was laid to rest in its burial chamber in the main pyramid.

ACTIVITY: From the description, trace the course the king's funeral procession would have taken from his Valley Temple to his burial chamber in the pyramid on the plan above.

# Animal Mummies and the Serapeum

Humans were not the only creatures to be mummified in Ancient Egypt. The Serapeum at Saqqara is just one of many catacombs containing the mummified remains of animals and birds. Discovered in 1851 by the famous French archaeologist Auguste Mariette, its crypts house enormous coffins hewn from single granite blocks, specially shaped to hold the mummies of the sacred Apis bulls.

*An Apis bull was worshipped as the living incarnation of the god Ptah.*

## THE SERAPEUM

The Serapeum was extended by Prince Khaemwese, one of the many sons of Rameses II. As a high priest of Ptah, Khaemwese was in charge of caring for the Apis bulls. Some people believe a mummy found in the Serapeum is that of Khaemwese, who died before he could inherit his father's throne.

*Mummified animals were sometimes placed in bronze coffins like the one on the left.*

Some animals were associated with certain gods. People might purchase a mummified animal to take to a temple as an offering to a particular god. When some of these mummies were unwrapped in recent times, a few were found to be fakes. There were obviously some dishonest mummy dealers around!

Activity: Can you guess what animals have been mummified inside these bandages? Clue: one is a cat, another an ibis, the third a baboon, the fourth a snake and the fifth an Apis bull.

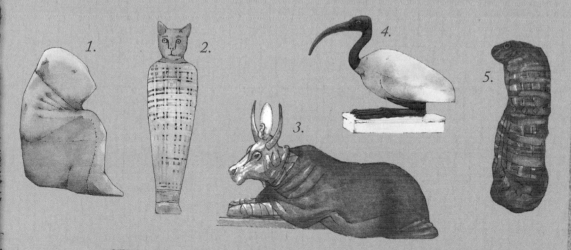

1.

2.

3.

4.

5.

ANSWERS: 1. Baboon 2. Cat 3. Apis Bull 4. Ibis 5. Snake

# Lesson 30
# The Amarna Heresy

The Amarna period, during the rule of the 'heretic Pharaoh' Akhenaten, continues to puzzle and divide scholars. During this time, Amenhotep IV banned the worship of Ancient Egypt's many traditional gods in favour of the worship of just one god — the Aten. He changed his name to Akhenaten and set up a brand new capital city half-way between Memphis and Thebes at Tel el Amarna called Akhetaten, the 'horizon of the Aten'.

### KING AKHENATEN

In representations of him from the Amarna period, Akhenaten has an unusual appearance — his head is very elongated, for example. This has led some scholars to wonder if he suffered from some kind of physical deformity. Others believe that this art style — like so much else in the reign of this extraordinary king — was distinctive in a drastic break from tradition, and that there was nothing wrong with Akhenaten's physique.

This sketch in the Amarna style shows a relief of Akhenaten that was found on one of the walls of the capital city that he built, Akhetaten. It shows the king, his wife, Nefertiti, and their daughters worshipping the Aten, which is represented on the relief as the rays of the sun.

## WHAT BECAME OF AKHENATEN

When Akhenaten died, it didn't take long for the country to return to the old religion and former capital city. Later generations reacted violently against this heretic king, and his name and monuments were defaced to obliterate all trace of him. The fact that we remember the boy-king who was probably Akhenaten's son as Tutankhamun, "Living Image of Amun", (and not by his original name of Tutankhaten, "Living Image of the Aten'" shows how immediate and complete the reversal of the Akhenaten's Amarna revolution was.

ACTIVITY: Names were very important in ancient Egypt. Amenhotep IV ("Amun is at peace") changed his name to Akhenaten ("Servant of the Aten"). Using your knowledge of Egyptian gods, can you work out which of these names belong to the Amarna period?

1. Meritaten ("The Aten's Beloved")
2. Ptahhotep ("Ptah is at Peace")
3. Sithathor ("Daughter of Hathor")
4. Ankhesenpaaten ("May she Live for the Aten")

ANSWER: 1 and 4.

# Appendix 1
# A Chronology of Egyptian History

NOTE: Dates in the history of Ancient Egypt are usually estimates, especially for the earliest periods.

PRE-DYNASTIC PERIOD, 5000–3200 BC

ARCHAIC PERIOD, 3200–2650 BC

2950 BC Earliest written texts at Abydos.

2900 BC Reign of NARMER (Menes?), first king of United Egypt. The country's capital is established at Memphis.

OLD KINGDOM, 2650–2150 BC

2630 BC Step Pyramid of ZOSER, the first monumental stone building in the world, built by Imhotep.

2550 BC Great Pyramid of KHUFU, followed by the pyramids of KHAEFRA and MENKAURA at Giza.

2150 BC The death of PEPI II, after lengthy 94-year reign, marks the end of the Old Kingdom.

FIRST INTERMEDIATE PERIOD, 2150–2040 BC

2150 BC Central power breaks down, leading to political chaos in Egypt. The kingdom is no longer united under one king.

MIDDLE KINGDOM, 2040–1750 BC

2040 BC The Theban MENTUHOTEP II becomes king of a reunited Egypt. Thebes becomes the new capital.

1750 BC The Middle Kingdom comes to a gradual end, as 13th-dynasty kings lose control of the country.

SECOND INTERMEDIATE PERIOD, 1750–1550 BC

1650 BC Foreign Hyksos rulers, who built a kingdom in the north around Avaris, capture Memphis.

1540 BC KAMOSE, king of Thebes, leads his army in a raid on the city of Avaris.

NEW KINGDOM, 1550-1070 BC

1550 BC King AHMOSE reunites Egypt at the start of the New Kingdom.

1500 BC THUTMOSIS I initiates the Valley of the Kings and founds the village at Deir El-Medina.

1480 BC Queen HATSHEPSUT ascends the throne.

1450 BC Under THUTMOSIS III Egyptian rule extends as far as the Euphrates river in the west.

1350 BC AMENHOTEP IV renames himself AKHENATEN, bans the worship of Egypt's old gods in favour of the Aten, and builds a new capital at Akhetaten.

1330 BC The cults of the old gods are restored under TUTANKHAMEN. Thebes becomes the capital of Egypt once again.

1275 BC RAMESES II fights the Hittites at the Battle of Kadesh. He builds many monuments to himself, including the temple at Abu Simbel.

1180 BC RAMESES III repels the invasion of the Sea Peoples. He is the last great Pharaoh of Egypt.

LATE NEW KINGDOM, 1070-712 BC

1070 BC The lessening power of the King leads to a loss of central control and Assyrian domination.

THE LATE PERIOD, 712-332

664 BC PSAMTEK I reunites Egypt, but it eventually falls to Persian, then Graeco-Roman kings.

GRAECO-ROMAN PERIOD, 332 BC-AD 395

332 BC ALEXANDER invades Egypt. Subsequently Egypt is ruled by the Ptolemys, the last of whom was CLEOPATRA VII.

# Appendix 2
## A Brief History of Egyptology

The first historians and archaeologists to be fascinated by Ancient Egypt were the Ancient Egyptians themselves. Travellers and tourists from the Old Kingdom onwards left traces of their presence at sites of historical interest, and some monuments were positively covered with Ancient Greek and Roman graffiti. European interest in Egypt began to develop after Napoleon's armies opened up the country in the early 19th century, and the scholars or 'savants' who travelled with Napoleon began recording the many wonderful things that they found.

**Giovanni Battista Belzoni**
**1778 – 1823**

*Belzoni shipped back to England many fine pieces of statue but his methods often resulted in damage.*

**Auguste Mariette**
**1821 – 1881**

*Auguste Mariette excavated many sites and founded the Antiquities Service and Egyptian Museum.*

**Amelia B. Edwards**
**1831 – 1892**

*Amelia Edwards wrote an account of her journey to Egypt and founded the Egypt Exploration Fund.*

**William Matthew Flinders Petrie**
**1853 –**

*Flinders Petrie developed many new archeological methods, such as using pottery in 'sequence dating'.*

**Howard Carter**
**1874 –**

*Howard Carter made a name for himself by finding and excavating the tomb of Tutankhamen.*

# A CHRONOLOGY OF EARLY EGYPTOLOGY

1400 BC The prince who was to become Thutmosis IV clears away the sand that has built up around the Sphinx.

1280 BC Prince Khaemwese, son of Rameses II, has inscriptions carved on some of the ancient monuments at Saqqara, to record that he restored them in his father's name.

450 BC Greek historian Herodotus writes a contemporary account of Ancient Egypt in "The Histories".

300 BC The Egyptian priest Manetho writes a "History of Egypt", dividing his lists of the kings into 30 dynasties.

1150 AD An Iraqi doctor, Abd el'Latif, writes of his journey around the ancient sites of Egypt.

1639 AD English mathematician John Greaves makes the first scientific survey of the Giza Plateau.

1745 AD The Reverend Richard Pococke publishes a two-volume account of his voyage to Egypt.

1790 AD James Bruce publishes his "Travels to Discover the Source of the Nile."

1798 AD Napoleon's ships arrive with a corps of 167 scholars, who aim to record every detail of the country in "La Description de L'Egypte".

1822 AD Frenchman Jean François Champollion writes his "Lettre à M. Dacier", which outlines the method for translating hieroglyphs.

The Bennu Bird,
January 5th 1927

My Dearest Niece and Nephew,

   Now that you have read my book you should know a
something about Egyptology and about the history of
Ancient Egypt. One of the reasons it is so exciting is
that egyptologists from museums and universities all
over the world are making new discoveries all the time.
Without their work many priceless antiquities and finds
that help us understand the lives of people who lived
many thousands of years in the past might be lost.

   For example, in order to control the flooding of the
Nile, the Egyptian authorities have had to build a dam
across the river near the first cataract at Aswan. As
the water has risen behind this dam it has began to
cover many important ancient sites, such as the Temple
of Philae. Without rescue work temples such as this may
be lost forever. So if you plan to go on to become
professional egyptologists when you grow up, I will
give you every encouragement!

   Your loving Aunt,       Emily

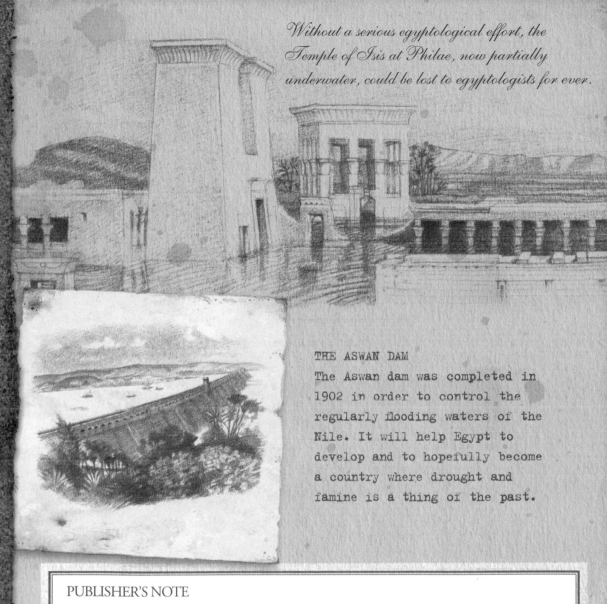

*Without a serious egyptological effort, the Temple of Isis at Philae, now partially underwater, could be lost to egyptologists for ever.*

THE ASWAN DAM
The Aswan dam was completed in 1902 in order to control the regularly flooding waters of the Nile. It will help Egypt to develop and to hopefully become a country where drought and famine is a thing of the past.

PUBLISHER'S NOTE

We have reproduced Miss Emily Sands journal much as it was discovered, so that it tends to reflect Egyptology as it was understood in 1926. However, there are a great many excellent modern books which will bring the reader up to date. One interesting fact is that the Temple of Isis at Philae that Miss Sands refers to was finally saved from the waters of the Nile when the Aswan High Dam was built – it was moved stone by stone onto a higher island nearby, as was the Temple of Abu Simbel, which also had to be reconstructed at a higher level.

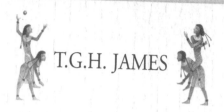

# T.G.H. JAMES

8 March 2005

Dear Reader,

Emily Sands was not a trained Egyptologist, but she had read a lot about Ancient Egypt, met important scholars, and attended many lectures on Egyptian subjects. She clearly knew a great deal, but perhaps not quite as much as she thought she did. The fruits of her knowledge are in this book. If you have enjoyed it, and want to know more, even more than Emily Sands, or even become an Egyptologist, then go as often as you can to museums where there are Egyptian antiquities, read some of the many useful books now available in good bookshops and libraries, and sometimes write little essays about things you have seen and enjoyed. You may not become a professional Egyptologist, but you will always be able to enjoy Egypt and its wonderful antiquities.

With good luck and best wishes,

*FGH James*

Formerly Keeper of Egyptian Antiquities at the British Museum